SHELBY THE SHARK

JENNY SCHREIBER

Shelby the Shark: Exploring the Secrets of the Great White Shark, Beginner Reader

©2023 Jenny Schreiber

Jenny Schreiber
Star Valley, WY 83110

In Association with
Elite Online Publishing
63 East 11400 South #230
Sandy, UT 84070
EliteOnlinePublishing.com

ISBN: 978-1-956642-91-9 (Paperback)
ISBN: 978-1-956642-92-6 (Hardback)

SHELBY THE SHARK

Meet Shelby
the great white shark

Shelby is a big fish
that lives in the ocean.

She is known as the
"great white"
because she has a big,
white belly.

She has tough skin called "cartilage" instead of bones.

Shelby is a very
fast swimmer.

Shelby has a lot of sharp teeth that help her catch food.

Shelby likes to eat fish, seals, and sometimes even dolphins.

Shelby has a special sense called "smell" that helps her find food in the water.

Shelby has amazing eyesight and can see really well underwater.

Great white sharks
are bigger than most
other sharks,
and some can grow
as long as a school bus!

Shelby has a special fin on her back that sticks out of the water when she swims.

Shelby likes to explore
things in the ocean,
she is very curious.

Shelby can jump out
of the water,
which is called
"breaching."

Shelby is not friendly
to humans and it's
best to stay away
from great white sharks.

Even though Shelby
may look scary,
she is important
for the ocean ecosystem.

When Shelby gives birth
to a baby shark,
they are called "pups."

Great white sharks
have been around
for a very long time,
even before dinosaurs!

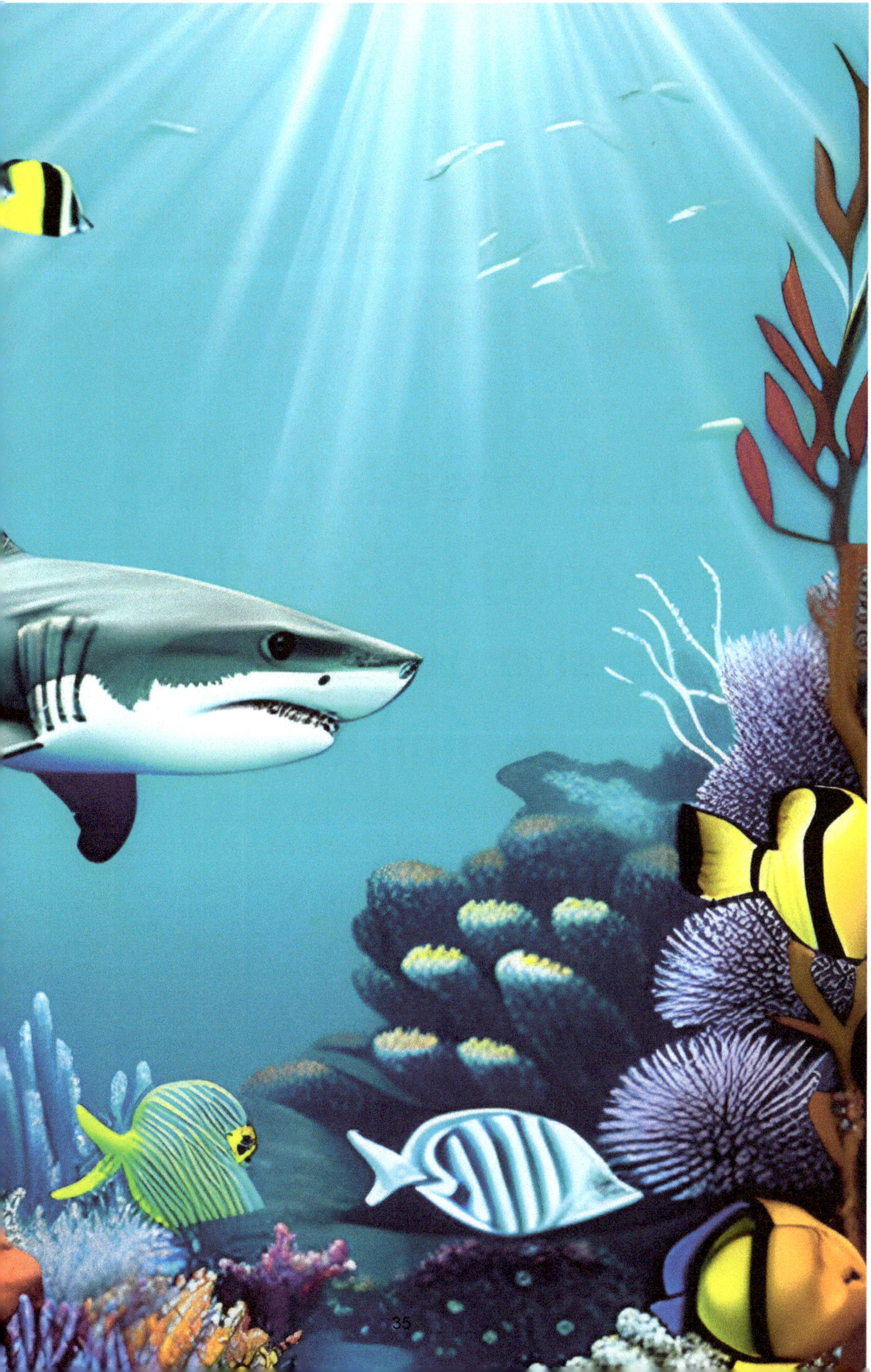

Shelby needs to keep
moving to breathe,
so she never stops
swimming.

Shelby can sense electrical signals from other animals, helping her find prey.

Scientists study great white sharks to learn more about them and how to protect them.

Shelby and her
great white shark
friends live in the ocean
near Australia,
South Africa,
and California.

The End

Find More books by Jenny Schreiber

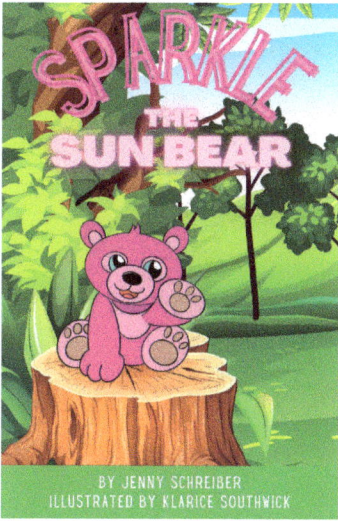

Sparkle the Sun Bear

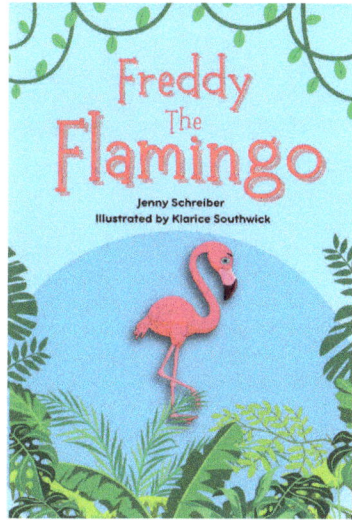

Freddy the Flamingo

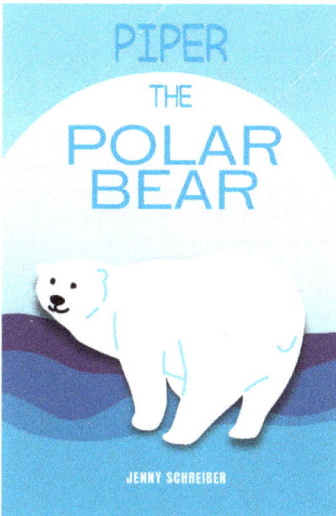

Piper the
Polar Bear

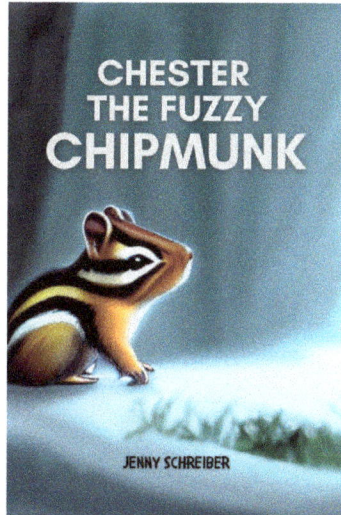

Chester the
Fuzzy Chipmunk

Animal Facts Children's Book Series

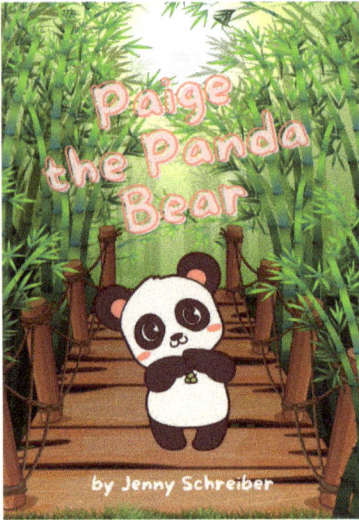

Paige the
Panda Bear

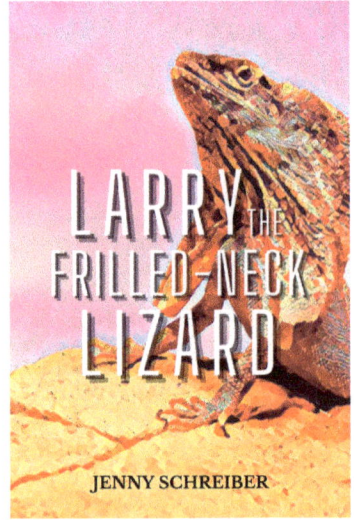

Larry the
Frilled-Neck Lizard

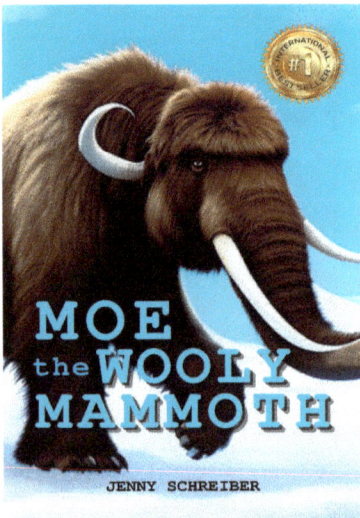

Moe the
Wooly Mammoth

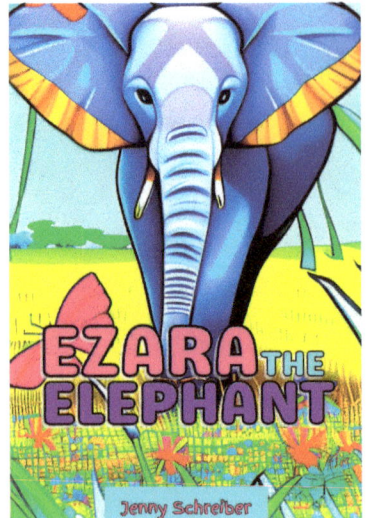

Ezara the
Elephant

www.ingramcontent.com/pod-product-compliance
Lightning Source LLC
Chambersburg PA
CBHW052123030426
12335CB00025B/3091